One 'n Done #13

My Heart, Hides

Poems by
Jimmy Cullen

Published by

Copyright 2026 Jimmy Cullen
All rights reserved.
Published by Read Furiously - Trenton, NJ. First Edition.

ISBN: 978-1-960869-26-5
LCCN: 2026934106

Poetry
Memoir
Mental Health
LGBTQIA+

In accordance with the U.S. Copyright Act of 1979, the scanning, uploading, and electronic sharing of any part of this book without the permission of the publisher or creator is forbidden.

No parts of this work were created using AI or any generative program. Use of its content within data models or AI learning programs of any kind is strictly forbidden.

For more information on *My Heart Hides* or Read Furiously, please visit readfuriously.com. For inquiries, please contact info@readfuriously.com.

Read: **[v]** The act of interpreting and understanding language, symbols, and the written word.

Furiously: **[adv]** To do something with excitement and passion.

Read Often. Read Well. Read Furiously

Awaiting Your Arrival

I awake in my bedroom
Alone
Silent
Patiently waiting for his appearance
Who knows what will happen
If he shows up tonight
Or in the morning
As time ticks on
I lose my ability to hope
My ability to see the light at the end of the tunnel
Time continues to push forward
That's what it means to exist
Kylie plays in my mind
Hoping that through my door
He will come and save me

Never Ending Journey

My last breath
Too heavy
To hold in
Filled with so much anxiety
I couldn't believe what relief would come
From the exhale
Light shines dimly
Highlighting the contours of my sinful face
I can't believe what has happened to me
Please don't judge
I'm only human
Behind I leave a world of regret
Before me is a world unknown
Is there any real God

Truly

No longer physical

I float into the universe
Hoping to find love
Hoping to find understanding

To Be

As another episode fades
A light becomes visible in the darkness
I run towards it
Hoping I won't fall again

The candles are lit in the chapel
Filled with loved ones
Praying for my return
The ending of his terror

Beyond the manicured gardens
I walk along the hall of mirrors
Finally capturing a glimpse of myself
How could something so worn look so good

At last I reach my bed chamber
I jump into bed wanting no more of this mania

I want to rule with my heart in my hands
I just want to be understood

Forever & Ever

As another day ends
A new night begins
I rest my crown of thorns
Hoping to dream of you
Wishing you were here with me
I call out in the night
For you to appear
To save me from the monotony
The endless cycle of life
In this physical world
At night I dream of stars
With them I can find my way
To my rightful place
Without fear
But it's done with a heavy heart
For I don't want to do this alone

Delightful World

Always give
Never receive
The time of self-nurturing
Never reveals itself to me
Like seeing the other side of the moon

What can follow in unfulfilled quests
To further my consciousness
While being unconscious
No one can tell me where I can go
Only that my mission is to help others
than myself

When can I fulfill me
To have satisfaction
A moment or feeling

Lasting more than a mere second
Can I get a glimpse of what's promised

Or shall I remain unconscious in this delightful existence

Casualties

Fake smiles
All for what
Is it helping you
Does it bring serenity
Will it increase endorphins
All the money you've spent
The bills that weren't even yours
Brought anxiety and shame
Those tears you call out for
That's what you need
Money can't buy emotion
It just covers it up

Making My Way

Your words aren't unique
They've been said a million times before
Acting like prima donnas
You don't know your ass from your elbow
Please keep in mind I exist
Everything you're experiencing
I've already experienced
You are not the golden child
Things don't easily come your way
I've worked harder than most to make my way
You're still young and naïve
You act as if you're more exhausted than others
Well I'm exhausted with my life
I'm exhausted with making my way
I'm exhausted with you

To Be Divine

How could you do this to me
I was doing fine on my own
All was dormant
I was existent
But silent

Now you've hit me hard
Large fragments of my body separate
I lost my shell
My essence is revealed
No longer can I rest

Because of you
I must shine
I must create my own galaxy
A place where I can see my fragments grow
Watching what the universe always had in mind

A Text To Mom

Through the years
My body has had many fevers
Not from external sources
Only from the inside

I grew up in confusion
Some pushed me one way
Others kept me in a neutral position
I couldn't take it anymore

Out of my body
Light shines
Pieces of me split
They have separated
Creating particles only God could know

The universe is my home
My multiple births
Climaxes

Have led me to this point of destruction
I was a star lying dormant
Now I shine for all to see

The End to the Beginning

It was really hard at first
To acknowledge my shine
The power that dwells within it

The love that seeps through my rays
Saturates the spherical particles
Orbiting my light

What could seem like a chore
Is more of a privilege than curse
For my love knows no bounds

Sadly one day I know my shine shall dim
My particles will perish
My heart will cease to beat

Can't Dim My Shine

I'm free falling from the garden
Instead of roses
I fall into a bed of stars
A place where infinity meets mortality

Gone is the black and white of the garden
Gone is the silvery light of the moon
Now I bask in the rays of the universe
Now I become a star amongst stars

Powers beyond my imagination seize control
The light I radiated created my new role
Now a dormant star about to explode
When I shine, will it blind you on earth

Mental Dysmorphia

So here I am
Waiting for the garden brush
Whistling to a tune locked inside
What can be done about this dysmorphia
When will I ever be enough for myself
I have to be honest too
There's more than one of me
But which one do I please
A constant cycle of never ending abuse
Who do I answer to
Who will think I am enough
Who will be there at the end
Waiting for me
In the garden

Particles

Those around me
Have no clue
How lonely it is
To shine alone
No one to call my own

These particles have plans of their own
They have one another to love
Revolving around each other
Encircling me

I guess I'm not alone
But I feel no joy to shine
A light that gives
And never receives

Starry Night

Bittersweet this world is
I find myself anticipating the night
To finally be free of my body
To say goodnight to the toils of my mind
As my head hits the pillow
I awake in a bed of stars
Neither up nor down
Just existing in a cosmic heaven
Sadly the stars begin to fade
I return to my body
Waking up to a bitter world
Where no love is in sight

Beyond Black & White

What power night brings
Moments of pleasure
Tales of yesteryear

The moon highlights the setting
A small garden
Having no light of its own
My love, the moon
Is illuminated by the rays of a great force
The sun

Together we can roam the garden
Find truth
Evoke meaning
Search for what we want most

I no longer fear the night
I no longer am chained to my garden
Now I can be free to find what I'm looking for

Now I can see a world beyond the black and white

We Shall See

I had such a hold on things
I did everything right
Dieted right
Slept right
Why does this have to come so quickly
Holding on to my comforter
I try to rest my mind and body
To no avail
Voices from the past creep in
I shut my eyes
Trying to focus on the sound of the television
Nothing can drown out those voices
They are having discussions with each other
I hear no words–just noise
What personality will take control
Sleep is erratic
Who will show their talons
Who will claw their way out of my body
And into existence

Make It Stop (Who Am I)

Make it stop
I cried into the unending darkness
Why can't I go back
Back to a time when I was stable
Where you didn't have to jump-start my mind
I loosely remember a time like that
I took it all for granted
Nothing but wastefulness and pure greed
I spin this world like a quarter
Never knowing when it will stop
Which side will it fall on
Which side will be revealed
Who am I

To Be At Peace

Thunder in the distance
The sun's light dissipates
Dark clouds roll in
It begins to rain

Once again I am trapped
In my garden of delights
The rain saturates all of me
Trapping my soul
My personality in this wet hell

My roses are being pummeled
By the ferocity of this natural upset
Hope seems unreachable
Will it ever end
At last

The thunder ceases
The sunlight appears

No clouds in sight
My soul is at peace again

Fall From Grace

At this point
I'm at the edge of euphoria
I've gathered flowers in the garden
Danced under the rays of the silvery moon
My heart raced with such a power
I almost combusted

Now something has changed
The moon shines but doesn't shine on me
My flowers have wilted
My heart beats slowly
Almost to the point of death

I lay in my bed
Wondering what I did wrong
To receive such a horrible fall from grace
Why can't life be one big high
That's not what God/universe intended

What shall I do now that the euphoria has gone

Lilies of My Valley

My mind is crowded
Like a Monet painting
With hundreds of lilies
A bounty of personalities

Each one comes with its own singularities
Represented by very sharp
Bright petals
They last forever
Outwitting my dominance

What energy will I release when I pass
Will I enter into the next world
Will these lilies die with my body
Time will tell
Death

Dream Maker

When the day is done
A long night follows
You reflect upon your day
Wishing things to remain the same
Some things to be changed

You prepare your bed
Engage in your nightly rituals
To ensure you can rest soundly
For the night is long
Your mind has a journey to complete

As I lay down
I ask one question
Will I ever be the same
Closing my eyes I count to ten
Hoping for an endless dream again

The Journey Within

What's the trouble
You've passed many obstacles
Climbed every mountain
To get where you are today
Saying goodbye isn't easy
You had to say it many times
To those you loved
To those who tried to dim your shine

It's no wonder you are the way you are
Believe in what you believe
To burn a light so bright
It touches the souls you've come into contact with

At the end of the day
You sleep soundly
Keeping in mind
The journey starts here
Finding you is a journey within

My Heart (It Hides)

Just when I thought I was getting ahead
I spiral, leaving my heart in an unknown place
How am I living without its rhythm
Breathing without my daily dose of hysteria
I steady my path to destruction
Little by little I lose normal concepts
Temporality becomes a blur
I cannot say hello or goodbye
My presence just resides
While my heart hides

Worry

I just want you to know my name
To understand where I'm coming from
Where I'm at currently
I could give two shits about my reputation
It doesn't matter in the long run

You see these bruises
You see these scars
I've been walking on this path for too long
When will I come to that door
Will it open for me

Slowly I regain focus
I'm in her bedroom
Watching her dry her hair
Talking to me like she always has
My silence is the beginning of the end
I'll just pretend this never happened

I don't want anyone to worry
Just know my name

When I Stopped... Believing

Christmas lights twinkle
In a black crystal night
I wander through the endless maze of memory
Another year has passed
Another Christmas without you
And many more to come
I know her heart is broken and cannot be fixed
So many things we do to fill in the gap you left
On the surface are smiles
Beneath lies bloody memories
I cannot believe
I won't believe in Christmas magic anymore

If Pillows Could Talk

The day is done
The night begins
Where will my dreams take place
Will I see the future
Will I see you

The day is through
The night is long
I begin to wonder if this adjustment will do
I begin to think of you
The anniversary is near

The sun has set
The moon has risen
My heart beats slowly
Letting my bodily functions come to a rest
Giving my mind the option to seek comfort
Or destroy every good thing about today

A Fallen Lover

I walk alone
Telling myself lies
Filling my head with dreams
Dreams that will never come true

Some days I believe in my positive thoughts
Some days I have anger towards them
I've been left before
Alone on Earth
Many men fading to black
Dissolving into the Earth

Today I eat my lunch
Think about you
About me
Love

Delicate
It's not easy
To talk to you
Delicate is the floor beneath us
One misstep
The whole world shatters

You're on a roll
Badgering me with helpless words
I just want to exist
In a better place

So long to empathy
Say hello to curt words
Cold shoulders
And screams

To Be With Him

It's been too long
I haven't had contact in ten years
Appropriate contact
Marked by a date

Inside my past is clouding my heart
This new beau makes me feel safe
Calm
Collected

Whenever I don't hear from him
My heart breaks
My past lovers have tainted my heart
Holding together – I stand
Letting nothing ruin this wonderful
Connection

When conversations become short
I don't know if I'm not in his favor

It created a wall of anxiety
Squeezing my heart
I talk to myself often
To keep me off the ledge
To see that he could be it
I've traveled many years
Many lifetimes
To find someone I can feel safe with

A Financial Mess

I could buy anything
Anything in this world
But it won't fill
The hole you left behind
In my heart

I hope I'm doing you proud
There's so much more we could've shared
Maybe see me get married
Get the stability I always craved
That's what you gave me
Before you left

No one will get our humor
I'm glad we share that together
I think of you throughout these days
Hoping you are there behind me
Rooting me on...

Queer

The door has closed
A window has opened
I rest peacefully on my bed
Thinking of nothing

Slowly it becomes queer
My body is shaking
Things become foggy
The veil begins to drop

Covering my face
I manage to speak
"Will this be the end of me"
Holding tight, I let go

Savage

There is a forest
A place of darkness with no end in sight
He calls it home
Behind the lush foliage
Hidden in the shadows
Is a man
Trapped by his own doings
Searching for truth
For himself
I'd like to introduce you to
The Savage

Private Property

The showboi walks
He talks
But never tells his truth
In the words
You'll find him
Hidden somewhere
In the garden

Waiting to be discovered
Is his piety
The virtues he once had
His voice
Which has become stifled, mute
When will we hear his voice

Beyond the garden
Lies a land undiscovered
A land to be uncovered
A treasure so great

His truth
Will be found
One day

Can't Keep Me Down

You thought you could strip me of my title
My religion
Leaving me to fall into a hole to hell

Fortunately for me
I rose above the hate crime
Like the creature that I am
I emerged from the lake of fire

Immortal
I use my words to ensnare my enemies
Demonstrating the true definition of
Queen
I'll make them regret what they've done to me
Housed in a palatial compound
White rooms
Floor to ceiling windows
Marie Antoinette would be envious

What was once a drab and pitiful existence
Has turned into one of simplistic opulence
No one can bring down my reign
No one can outwit the showboi

Goodnight Kisses

Feed me it says
I'm starving
You've deprived me of what I need
Pain
Grief
Sorrow
I never left
I've remained dormant
Only to await the freedom that I've been denied for so many years
Begin delusions
Begin grandeur
Begin to see life again as unbalanced
A place where it's black and white again
Try to sleep my pet
Close those eyes of yours
I'm only an inch away from you
Feed me what I need to survive
Let me control the chaos you contain yourself

Red Dodge

I couldn't believe it
I couldn't see it coming
Thinking you were indestructible
That we were immortal
Boy, was I wrong

Riding in the car
I couldn't feel anything
Numb to all natural emotions
Would I be like stone
Will I be like a stone for all my life

Climbing the steps
I still couldn't believe this was happening
The silence of the hallways was deafening
Emphasizing the purpose of this building
It's transient state
We've reached the doors

Finally my heart became warm
Passing the rooms of others
Whose hearts cannot say enough
I love you, I love you, I love you
We have reached his room
A single glass partition separating us
from him

All my emotions come to the front
I let out a cry and finally break down
How could I be mad at him
How could I not love him
He's my daddy
The leader of our pact

Please don't go daddy
I repeated between tears
What will happen without you
I wished hard to take your place
You have so much to offer

I'll always remember the red dodge
The joy I felt seeing you
Making a special trip
A time I'll treasure forever

So if you can hear me
When it's my time
Come pick me up in that red dodge
I look forward to seeing you
Again

Courage (What If)

The sun's rays
Shine on new opportunities
New avenues to pursue
The things I can't bring myself to face
Holding back
I cannot go another step
What if it leads me to another obstacle
What if it ends in being overcautious
One must champion the unknown
Open that door
Walk through
See what God has in store for you

Sunny Sunflower

Hold on to me
Sunflower girl
Hold on to you
Sunflower girl

Remembering when we had each other
The times we braved our worst storms
How we remained above mediocrity
No selfishness behind our actions

Hold on to me
Sunflower girl
Hold on to you
My sunflower girl

I couldn't tell you what was on my mind
You wouldn't have believed it — if you tried
What could I have said to you — a strong mother

How could I tell you I couldn't go on any longer

Hold on to me
Sunflower girl
I'm holding on to you
My sunny, sunny sunflower girl

I gotta break this chain
Nothing can break us apart
I will stand in the pouring rain
To see your face — one more time

Hold me tight sunflower girl
I'll hold you my sunflower girl
Our love will continue to thrive
Even though you are not by my side

Lights
Up above
Shine down
On those you loved

Rare Breed

The sunrises
Illuminating my bedroom
No servants
No lords
No one

The sun shines onto my ornate environment
Hitting the crystals
The sun dances across my quarters
Producing thousands of rainbows

I'm glad no one is up yet
I can just enjoy being me – a human
Hoping to enjoy the simple pleasures
Instead of listening to matters of state

Lying in a sea of rainbows
I feel recognized for being a rare breed

I bring something special
A unique kind of attitude rarely seen
In this corrupt court I call life

So as I prepare for the daily onslaught
I just hold on to this private moment
Knowing, I'm more than a Queen
That God has more in store for me

Light My Fire

You ignite my spirit
No longer dwelling in the shadows
Becoming present in the moment

The speaker brings to mind the many
wonders of psychosis
I dance in circles
Throwing roses around the Virgin Mother

From one to another
The songs touch upon my bouts
I'm having one right now

Slowly I lift the veil to reveal
Someone just like me
Checked in
While I checked out

Express

You're not around
I keep lying to myself that you're with me
Even though there are "signs" telling me you're there

I can't go on pretending that I fully grieved
I was too doped up on pills to feel anything
Now with a lower dosage
I can feel what I couldn't
These past two years

I loved you from the start
I was the one tearing us apart
But what kept us together was faith
Faith in the human spirit
Faith that can continue beyond death

Faith in our love of family
So I can't say right now what I'm thinking
But I'm thinking that this will be
An unusual grieving period

You Can't Tell Me I'm Wrong

I fear the night
I fear the day
Without hope
I feel as if I'm stuck in hell

I fear the death of my mother
I fear the death of my sister
Without them
Life would mean nothing to me

So I'll take that tranquilizer
To help stop these fears
But it doesn't work at all
I am so far removed from the world
There's no peace in the kingdom
There's no peace in my mind

The Grand Unveiling

I step into a pool of water
Toe first
Depending on the temperature
I shall walk deeper into the water
Until fully submerged
Diamonds and all

It's a process I go through personally
To find myself
To reinvent myself
A stronger persona
Hiding myself deep inside
Not wanting to get hurt

As I transform into a new "me"
I lose my diamonds, my feathers
The tears I had on before
Vanish beneath the water's surface
Gasping for air, I rise to the surface

I open my eyes
Take a deep breath in
I am the new persona
The raw, unfiltered self
I guess it's my time to shine
Let everyone in on the secret
To show the real me

Feeling So Alone

They're around me again
Moving in on my moment of peace
They strangle me
I claw at my face
Trying to free myself from the veil of depression
I begin to suffocate
I claw away at the veil
In reality
I'm scraping the skin off my face
I wish to die
Never wanting this to happen again
Knowingly so
I regain my composure
Submit to the power of depression
Slipping slowly into the blackness of it all

Fooling The World

He can hear the crowd
Chanting his name
He walks down the hall
Adorned with his armor
A bounty of peacock feathers

The chants grow louder
As he approaches the stairs
Leading to the spotlight
To a world he has fooled
When will he reveal his true self

The platform rises
He strikes a pose
Dominating the stage
He wishes he could hide
But he is hiding

Dazzling the crowd
He smiles with ferocity
Shines violently
And thinks to himself
Who am I

What Lies Beyond The Curtain

Applause
Whistles
Cheers
Everything a showboi wants but doesn't need
As the lights fade
The curtain closes
Leaving him crestfallen

Strutting towards the dressing room
The showboi sheds his peacock feathers
Removes his diamonds
Takes off his plastic smile
Finally he's reached the haven

Inside the showboi stares at himself in the mirror
Thinking about the past present and what has yet to come

People don't see beyond the glitter
Beyond the illusion he presents to them
It's a lonely life
Showboi
A life of loneliness and glamour

Keeping Me Afloat

There's something lurking
Beneath my skin
Deep below
Beyond the garden

I'm putting up a good fight
It continuously tries to dismantle me
I'm not giving up this time
Nothing can deter me

It's pulling me
Pushing me to act out
Pressuring me to speak
Out of turn

Why can't there be peace
In a tumultuous kingdom
Where happiness is scarce
And pain is in abundance

I close my eyes
Breathe in deep
And steady myself
Knowing
Like always
I'll survive

About the Author

A dedicated barista with the intention to be understood by the world, born in New York but raised in New Jersey, Jimmy has battled with mental illness all his life. Officially diagnosed with Bipolar I after his suicide attempt, since then he's been holding on to a steady job while trying to find the best avenue to express himself emotionally. Poetry has become his vehicle for navigating through tough waters and finding moments of enlightenment. His first collection, *Showboi: Too Deep Too Care* was released by Read Furiously in 2023. Jimmy looks forward to expressing himself to you. All you have to do is listen.

A Note to our Furious Readers

From all of us at Read Furiously, we hope you enjoyed our latest installment in our One 'n Done series, *My Heart, Hides*.

We pledge to donate a portion of these book sales to causes that are special to Read Furiously. These causes are chosen with the intent to better the lives of others who are struggling to tell their own stories.

Reading is more than a passive activity – it is the opportunity to play an active role within our world. Each cause has been researched thoroughly, discussed openly, and voted upon carefully by our team of Read Furiously editors.

To find out more about who, what, why, and where Read Furiously lends its support, please visit our website at readfuriously.com/charity

Happy reading and giving, Furious Readers!

Read Often, Read Well, Read Furiously!

More in the One 'n Done Series

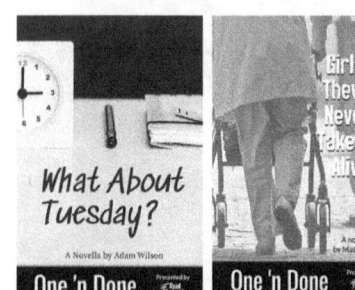

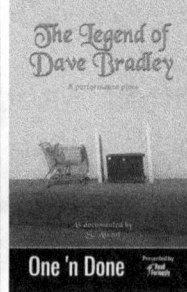

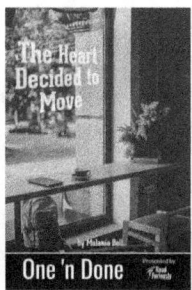

**Small Books. Big Impact.
Learn more about the series at
readfuriously.com/one**

www.ingramcontent.com/pod-product-compliance
Lightning Source LLC
LaVergne TN
LVHW012125070526
838202LV00056B/5863